TWO
CITIES

9 INTERACTIVE BIBLE STUDIES FOR
SMALL GROUPS AND INDIVIDUALS

ANDREW REID
AND KAREN MORRIS

Two Cities
Second edition
© Matthias Media 2009

First published 1993

Matthias Media
(St Matthias Press Ltd ACN 067 558 365)
PO Box 225
Kingsford NSW 2032
Australia
Telephone: (02) 9663 1478; international: +61-2-9663-1478
Facsimile: (02) 9663 3265; international: +61-2-9663-3265
Email: info@matthiasmedia.com.au
Internet: www.matthiasmedia.com.au

Matthias Media (USA)
Telephone: 724 964 8152; international: +1-724-964-8152
Facsimile: 724 964 8166; international: +1-724-964-8166
Email: sales@matthiasmedia.com
Internet: www.matthiasmedia.com

ISBN 978 1 921441 37 0

Cover design and typesetting by Lankshear Design Pty Ltd.

›› CONTENTS

›› HOW TO MAKE THE MOST OF THESE STUDIES

1. What is an Interactive Bible Study?

Interactive Bible Studies are a bit like a guided tour of a famous city. They take you through a particular part of the Bible, helping you to know where to start, pointing out things along the way, suggesting avenues for further exploration, and making sure that you know how to get home. Like any good tour, the real purpose is to allow you to go exploring for yourself—to dive in, have a good look around, and discover for yourself the riches that God's word has in store.

In other words, these studies aim to provide stimulation and input and point you in the right direction, while leaving you to do plenty of the exploration and discovery yourself.

We hope that these studies will stimulate lots of 'interaction'—interaction with the Bible, with the things we've written, with your own current thoughts and attitudes, with other people as you discuss them, and with God as you talk to him about it all.

2. The format

Each study contains five main components:

- short sections of text that introduce, inform, summarize and challenge
- a set of numbered study questions that help you examine the passage and think through its meaning
- sidebars that provide extra bits of background or optional extra study ideas, especially regarding other relevant parts of the Bible
- an 'Implications' section that helps you think about what this passage means for you and your life today
- suggestions for thanksgiving and prayer as you close.

3. How to use these studies on your own

- Before you begin, pray that God would open your eyes to what he is saying in the Bible, and give you the spiritual strength to do something about it.
- Work through the study, reading the text, answering the questions about the Bible passage, and exploring the sidebars as you have time.
- Resist the temptation to skip over the 'Implications' and 'Give thanks and pray' sections at the end. It is important that we not only hear and understand God's word, but respond to it. These closing sections help us do that.
- Take what opportunities you can to talk to others about what you've learnt.

4. How to use these studies in a small group

- Much of the above applies to group study as well. The studies are suitable for structured Bible study or cell groups, as well as for more informal pairs and triplets. Get together with a friend or friends and work through them at your own pace; use them as the basis for regular Bible study with your spouse. You don't need the formal structure of a 'group' to gain maximum benefit.

- For small groups, it is *very useful* if group members can work through the study themselves *before* the group meets. The group discussion can take place comfortably in an hour (depending on how sidetracked you get!) if all the members have done some work in advance.

- The role of the group leader is to direct the course of the discussion and to try to draw the threads together at the end. This will mean a little extra preparation— underlining the sections of text to emphasize and read out loud, working out which questions are worth concentrating on, and being sure of the main thrust of the study. Leaders will also probably want to work out approximately how long they'd like to spend on each part.

- If your group members usually don't work through the study in advance, it's extra important that the leader prepares which parts to concentrate on, and which parts to glide past more quickly. In particular, the leader will need to select which of the 'Implications' to focus on.

- We haven't included an 'answer guide' to the questions in the studies. This is a deliberate move. We want to give you a guided tour of the Bible, not a lecture. There is more than enough in the text we have written and the questions we have asked to point you in what we think is the right direction. The rest is up to you.

5. Getting started in Isaiah

Studying Isaiah is something of a daunting prospect. It is a huge book in every respect. It is big on length, on thematic breadth and grandeur, on complexity, and on importance. Isaiah has been described as the 'Romans' of the Old Testament, and one can see why. It is full of essential and profound biblical ideas, such as the sovereignty of God, sin, judgement, salvation and the new creation. With the possible exception of the Psalms, Isaiah is quoted or alluded to in the New Testament more than any other Old Testament book.

With such a book before us, a detailed verse-by-verse study of every chapter is not the best way to grasp the meaning of Isaiah as a whole. That would require a very much thicker book of studies, and would leave us somewhat in danger of missing the forest for the trees. Instead, we'll be studying the nine key passages which, taken together, provide a solid understanding of Isaiah as a whole.

Whether you're meeting in a group or using this study book on your own, it would be a good idea at some stage to read right through Isaiah. Set aside a wet Sunday afternoon and read it in one sitting. If you can't manage this, you could try to read steadily through Isaiah while you're working through the studies—say, seven chapters a week, if you're doing the studies in a group over nine weeks.

We also suggest that, before you begin, you read appendix 1 to understand the historical context of Isaiah. It will be an enormous help in identifying many of the historical figures and events that are being referred to as the book unfolds. Make sure you read this appendix at least before you get to study 3.

If you would like to do any further reading on Isaiah, the best commentaries are those by John Calvin (hard to read these days but worth the effort) and the volume in the New International series by Oswalt. Barry Webb's commentary in the Bible Speaks Today series is excellent.

6. Bible translation

Previous studies in our Interactive Bible Study series have assumed that most readers would be using the New International Version of the Bible. However, since the release of the English Standard Version in 2001, many have switched to the ESV for study purposes. For this reason, we have decided to quote from and refer to the ESV text, which we recommend.

CHOOSING A CITY

[ISAIAH 1:1–2:4]

ISAIAH IS A VERY BIG BOOK. IT'S the kind of book that makes you feel uncomfortable just looking at it. Wouldn't it be good to get 'the big picture' of what it's all about before we start reading? One of the great things about Isaiah is that the first chapter introduces many of the big themes of the book. Reading Isaiah 1 is the best way to get into Isaiah. So without any further ado, let's dive straight in and have a look at it.

Read Isaiah 1:1–2:4.

1. Without spending too much time, jot down the big ideas or themes that strike you as important.

A tale of two cities

PEOPLE TELL THE STORY OF THE Bible in lots of different ways. Some focus on the history of the Jewish nation; others talk about the theme of salvation; yet others speak about God's promises to his people. Each of these ways of talking about the Bible is helpful and true.

One way to tell the story of the Bible is as 'a tale of two cities' (to borrow the title of Charles Dickens' famous novel). The story of these two cities is the story of God dealing with his world and his people.

Babel is the first city of any size mentioned in the Bible (Gen 11:1-9). It lies on the plain of Shinar and is also known as 'Babylon'. Babel is famous for its humanism—that is, it is a city where the people are centrally concerned about themselves and their betterment. Babel epitomizes the self-centred human dream; it is a place where humans are in control, building a better world for themselves and determining their own future.

The Bible also presents a city where things are different—*Jerusalem*—known elsewhere as 'Zion' or the 'City of David'. Jerusalem was the city captured by God's great king, David. It became the resting place of the Ark of the Covenant—the sign of God's presence with his people. It is the city where the Temple of Solomon was built, consecrated and blessed with God's presence. It is God's city.

Two cities: Babel and Jerusalem. One devoted to humanity, the other ruled by God. One me-centred, the other God-centred. The two cities are images of two ways of life.

A book about Jerusalem

Isaiah is a book about Jerusalem. It begins and ends with Jerusalem and talks about it everywhere in between. And because Jerusalem is God's city, God has a dream for it. That dream is celebrated in the Psalms, in particular Psalms 46 and 48, where we see some of the characteristics of God's ideal city. (You might like to quickly read Psalm 48 to capture God's dream.)

The ideal Jerusalem of Psalm 48 stands in stark contrast to the city of Babel in Genesis 11. Jerusalem is clearly identified with God and has him at its heart. It is the place from which God rules his world; a place where the people of God live and rejoice.

Re-read Isaiah 1:1-2:4.

2. How is God's city described? What is life like in Jerusalem/Zion?

3. Summarize, as simply as you can, Isaiah's message to Judah and Jerusalem in these verses.

4. Outline the future of Jerusalem as described in this passage. Is everybody's future within the city the same?

Inside the walls

IN CHAPTER 1, ISAIAH TAKES US inside the walls of Jerusalem. As soon as we are inside it becomes quite obvious that the dream is not the same as the reality. In reality, Jerusalem is a place where:

- people don't know God (Isa 1:2-3)
- covenants/contracts are broken (Isa 1:4-9)
- people refuse to be God's people (Isa 1:10-12)
- twisted and perverted worship is carried out (Isa 1:11-14)
- wickedness, injustice and disobedience flourish (Isa 1:15-17, 21-23).

In short, *Babel has invaded Jerusalem, and human-centredness has pushed God out of his own city.* This is the situation addressed by Isaiah. He belongs to a community who rightly claim to be God's chosen people, and yet they are a people of "unclean lips" (Isa 6:5). They are a rebellious city. How can the Holy One of Israel dwell in the midst of a city like this?

He cannot. Isaiah goes on to tell us about the fate of Jerusalem. The city must be purified, and those who continue to resist God's rule will be destroyed. This is the main point of the first half of the book—Jerusalem has become defiled and is therefore doomed. This message reaches its climax in chapter 39, where the end of the city is promised.

Isaiah 40-66 addresses a destroyed Jerusalem and a nation in exile in Babylon. The message of these chapters is very different in tone from the first half of the book. The first half is mainly about judgement, with glimpses of salvation here and there. The second half is more about salvation, with reminders of judgement here and there. In Isaiah 40-66, although Jerusalem has been judged, the hope of a redeemed, ideal Jerusalem remains. God will again dwell in the midst of his people. Isaiah ends with a picture of God's goal being reached—a new heavens, a new earth and a new Jerusalem, in which right-eousness and peace dwell.

We will return to these majestic themes in due course. In the meantime, chapter 1 of Isaiah introduces us to many of these ideas. It functions as an introduction to the book as a whole and in some ways as an overview of it. Many of the ideas mentioned in it are repeated throughout the book. The contrast between the two cities, Babylon and Jerusalem, will arise time and again. It is a story that reminds us that God has a purpose—to complete a world centred on himself. This purpose will be accomplished. For those who align themselves with God's purpose, this will mean life, salvation and blessing. For others, who continue in human-centredness, this will mean death, judgement and curse.

We will eventually discover that, in a quite unexpected way, God will bring salvation and judgement together to achieve a stunning victory and the fulfil-ment of all his plans.

» Implications

- Look back over Isaiah 1. Imagine you are an Israelite hearing Isaiah speaking these words. What would your emotional reaction be? Why would you feel like this?

- How do the people of the 'rebellious city' show their allegiance? How are those who are loyal to the 'future Jerusalem' different?

- How do people around you show their allegiance to either city?

- How do you?

- God says that 'Jerusalem' is his future for his world. If this is where things are headed then what does it mean for you?

- What sort of actions should you take as a consequence?

» Give thanks and pray

- Give thanks to God for his promise of a new Jerusalem and for his promise that justice will one day be done.
- Pray for our world, which continues in rebellion against God. Pray people would hear God's call to repentance. (You might like to pray for one or two specific people or family members.)

HIDING FROM REALITY

[ISAIAH 2:5-22]

THERE IS NOTHING LIKE TRYING on a new pair of glasses. It's almost like being in a dream and then suddenly waking up. Everything is sharp, vivid, real. All the fuzziness disappears and reality slaps you in the face.

In Isaiah 2, the prophet Isaiah plays the part of the optician. He gets us to examine the sins of Israel and then he shoves newly adjusted spectacles onto our noses. The reality and source of Israel's sin lies exposed in a way it never was before. Look at the passage and you'll see that we mean.

Read Isaiah 2:5–22.

1. What words and phrases are repeated in the passage?

2. How do these repeated words and phrases contribute to the picture that Isaiah is painting of the day of God's judgement?

3. There are a number of words and phrases in verses 6-8 and 13-14 that need explanation because they are symbolic. Once we know the meaning of these symbols, the passage becomes clearer. Using these suggested explanations of the imagery, write a one-sentence summary of what each section means.

- **Fortune-tellers** (v. 6) and magic were strictly forbidden in Israel. The nations used these practices in an attempt to gain control of their destinies and to manipulate their gods. Israel was called upon to trust God and not to attempt to manipulate him or put him to the test.

- **Strike hands with the children of foreigners** (v. 6) means doing business with people from other nations. Doing business with foreigners often involved the recognition of the foreigner's gods.

   Write your own summary of verses 6-9:

- The **cedars of Lebanon** (v. 13) were large, spreading, coniferous trees that grew abundantly on Mount Lebanon. They were great wonders for Palestinians, who only knew the small and warped trees of the hill country.

- The **oaks** (v. 13) of Palestine are sturdy, hardwood trees which live to a great age. Bashan, to the East of the Jordan, was renowned for its groves of oak trees.

- Israelites feared the sea and therefore ships were a source of wonder and amazement for them. **Ships of Tarshish** (v. 16) probably refers to large, long-range Phoenician merchant boats that were used for the longest routes and acted as flagships of the fleets.

- **Mountains, hills, towers,** and **walls** (vv. 14-15) were symbols of power and security in Canaan.

   Write your own summary of verses 12-18:

4. Looking back over the passage, what is the essence of Israel's sin?

That day

THROUGHOUT THIS PASSAGE THERE are a number of references to *that day* or *the day of the Lord*. This sort of language is commonly used by the prophets, from Amos onwards. It is a shorthand way of talking about the day when God's goal for his world will be fulfilled through his intervention in history in a special way. On that day, God will come in all his splendour and the world will recognize that he alone has the right to be the world's centre of attention.

As God's special people, Israel looked forward to this day. They considered that this day would be a great day for them since it would mean vindication and blessing. God would punish all the nations who refused to recognize him and relate rightly to him, and he would bless the nation who did recognize him and live rightly with him (note the picture of this in Isaiah 2:1-4).

5. In light of this passage, do you think the Israelites should have been looking forward to that day? Why/why not?

Idolatry

THERE ARE TWO THEMES WHICH RUN through Isaiah 2: idolatry (vv. 6-9) and human pride (vv. 12-17). (Look back at your answers to the first three questions in this study. Do you agree?) In Isaiah's view, these are the two great shortcomings of Israel and they go together.

In verse 22, Isaiah tells the Israelites how to beat both problems in one go:

> Stop regarding man
> in whose nostrils is breath,
> for of what account is he? (Isa 2:22)

If we saw flagrant idolatry and pride, we wouldn't generally deal with it in this way. We would call for people to turn away from pride and to burn all their idols. Isaiah's approach is very different. His way of dealing with pride and idolatry is to tell God's people to turn away from human beings.

Isaiah lived in a society littered with idols. He also knew that idolatry was more serious than tiny figurines of gold with bulging eyes and emerald studded navels might suggest. Isaiah wasn't simply into tearing down any idol he could find. He wanted to dig down and find the root of the sin of idolatry. And he did find it. In verse 22, he unmasks the idol that lies at the root of all idols—human beings themselves.

The Bible's picture of humanity is clear. Humans are created beings, made by God out of the dust of the earth. Therefore the greatest form of idolatry is when humans make themselves greater than their creator; when the creature worships the creature rather than the creator. An idol is thus anything we use to try to be independent of God, or anything (or anyone) we devote ourselves to and become dependent on rather than God.

›› Implications

- If you were an Israelite hearing Isaiah speak this prophecy how would you react?

Read Psalm 14 and Isaiah 6:1–5.

- Given this information about God and humanity, why will the day of the Lord be a day of darkness for all people?

- It is clear from the New Testament that idolatry is as much a problem for us as for the Israelites (Gal 5:20; Col 3:5; 1 Pet 4:3; 1 John 5:21). What things do people turn to rather than God?

- What things do *you* turn to rather than God?

- What can you do to challenge your idols?

» Give thanks and pray

- Make a list of as many differences as you can between God and our idols. (It would be good to notice in particular the things that Isaiah says about God's character in this passage.) Turn these things into points of praise, giving thanks to God for what he is like.
- Ask God to help you to turn away from your idols and towards him.

» STUDY 3

FACING THE REAL KING

[ISAIAH 6]

ISAIAH 6 IS ONE OF THOSE CHAPTERS that you know must be very important, but seems too strange to really understand. Angels fly back and forth, or stand in significant postures; people kiss burning coals; trains fill temples.

Sometimes it is our approach to the passage that causes our difficulties. If, instead of reacting to the unusual imagery, we focus on the story that is being told, the meaning of the passage becomes much clearer.

There are a number of passages which provide possible parallels or background to Isaiah 6. In each case, compare the passage with Isaiah 6 and list the possible connections and parallels between them.

- Exodus 3
  (especially vv. 1-6)

- Psalm 47

- 1 Kings 22:1-28
  (especially vv. 19-20)

- Numbers 16:42-50

- Exodus 32
  (especially vv. 9-14)

Read Isaiah 6.

1. List words or phrases used to describe God and his activity (e.g. who is he? Where is he? What is he doing? etc.). What do each of these words or phrases imply about God's character?

Words about God	→ What do they tell us about God's character?
•	→
•	→
•	→
•	→
•	→
•	→

King Uzziah

ISAIAH'S VISION IN CHAPTER 6 comes at a crucial time in the history of the southern nation of Judah—the year in which King Uzziah dies. Uzziah (also known as Azariah) reigned during a time of relative peace and prosperity. It was a time of optimism and confidence. But the optimism was unwarranted. The end of the reign of Uzziah virtually coincided with the resurgence of an aggressive and militarily superior Assyria to the north.

Uzziah's reign was a mixture of the positive and **negative**. The writer of the book of 2 Kings classes him as one of the better kings of Judah. Yet in spite of his successes, Uzziah was a king noted for mocking God's holiness. It was in the year of his death that Isaiah had his vision of the true king of Israel—the Lord, high and lifted up; the God who is holy.

3. Describe, step by step, and in your own words, how Isaiah is sent out by God in verses 1-9a.

Negative aspects of Uzziah's reign

The writer of Chronicles tells us that Uzziah's leprosy was due to his pride. Uzziah stepped outside the proper bounds of kingship and offered incense in the temple. When confronted by the priests, he became angry and resisted their push for him to leave the temple precincts. As a result, God struck him with leprosy. The illness remained for the rest of his life, meaning he spent his life in quarantine and total exclusion from the temple. (For more details see 2 Kings 14:21-22, 15:1-7 and 2 Chronicles 26.)

4. Try to summarize verses 8-10 in your own words.

5. What is difficult about these verses? Why is it difficult?

6. Isaiah asks God a question in verse 11. Summarize God's answer (in vv. 11-13).

7. Now that you've worked from verses 9-13, go back to your summary of verses 1-9a. Add in any necessary steps needed to summarize the whole chapter.

God the king

THERE IS A SIGNIFICANT AMOUNT of 'kingship' language in this chapter. We are told about a human king, about God the king and about God seated on a throne, high and exalted. It is no accident that Isaiah has a vision of God as king. Throughout the Old Testament God is the creator of the world and therefore its king (e.g. Pss 47:1-2, 7-9; 103:19; 145:10-13). And even though the word 'king' doesn't occur in Genesis 1, it is the key idea—God has made the world and he rules it.

In the ancient world, an image of a god or a king was considered to repre-sent that god or king. In Genesis 1:27ff, human beings alone are created in God's image—they are the evidence that God is the lord or king over all creation. We are created in God's image to represent his kingship. But that is not all. Humans are also God's stewards, or trustees, called to exercise the rule of God, under the rule of God, over the lower orders of creation. By our dominion over creation, we act like representatives of God the king.

Not all is well in Eden, however. By Genesis 3, human beings decide they don't like living and ruling under the kingship of God. Our rejection of God results in two things:

1. God judges and punishes humanity (Genesis 3-11)
2. God acts to start again with humanity (Genesis 11:27-12:3).

In Genesis 12, God starts again by choosing one man (Abraham) who will become one nation (Israel). They will be God's special people through whom his promises will be fulfilled.

However, with such a dismal past, it is inevitable that we find ourselves asking of Abraham and his descendants, "How are they going? How are they reacting to God the king?" In the book of Samuel, we find out that the nation descended from Abraham is no different from all other human beings. They too reject God as king and seek independence.

How to treat a king

With this background, we can understand a bit more of Isaiah 6. Isaiah sees "*the* King, the LORD of hosts!" (v. 5). When he looks at the praising seraphs, he sees how the king should be treated. After his vision, Isaiah is painfully aware of how his nation has rejected God and his rule. Isaiah does the only thing a human can do when confronted with the sovereign God:

- He *acknowledges* that God alone has the right to be addressed as king.
- He *repents* of his own sinfulness and the sinfulness of his people (i.e. in making themselves kings).

- He *depends* upon God for forgiveness and cleansing.
- He *listens* to God (i.e. turns from independence to dependence).
- He *obeys* what he hears from God.

The kingship of God also helps us understand the second half of the chapter. Isaiah is told that his preaching will not make it easier for Israel to believe and repent. On the contrary, it will make it harder. This is because humans are independent beings at their core. Preaching about the rule of God often challenges people and hardens them, thus confirming them in their independence and in their fate.

Thy kingdom come

We can see the effects of Isaiah 6:9-10 in the ministry of Jesus. His ministry was concerned with the rule of God, as demonstrated in his attitudes and teaching. He quotes these verses to his disciples after telling the parable of the sower to a large crowd (Mark 4:1-20). Jesus taught that when he preached the message of God's kingship, he got two typical reactions:

1. rejection (immediately or delayed)
2. acceptance.

Using Isaiah 6 as support, Jesus went on to say that acceptance of the message only comes with the help of God. Without God, everyone will be blind to the truth and become hard of heart. But with God, through the gospel, we too have been given the 'secret of the kingdom of God'.

» Implications

- If people are independent at heart and preaching makes them more so, how can anyone turn back to God?

- Go back and look at Isaiah's response to God in chapter 6. Where would you place yourself in the process of responding to God the king?

- Isaiah acknowledged, repented, trusted, listened and obeyed. Which of these do you struggle with most?

- How can you work on this?

» Give thanks and pray

- Give thanks to God for the aspects of his character that you saw in question 1.
- Ask God to help you to treat him as the true king. (If it is appropriate in your group, you may like to ask God for forgiveness for some of the ways you reject him.)

STUDY 4

GOD'S DREAM

[ISAIAH 11]

A quick revision

ONE OF THE DIFFICULTIES IN reducing the whole of Isaiah to nine studies is that it is easy to lose the big picture of the book. A quick revision may help us to maintain our bird's-eye view of the whole while we look at individual passages. Let's remember how the first 12 chapters of Isaiah have fitted together.

Chapter 1 introduced the book by presenting the main themes and ideas that the rest of Isaiah would talk about in more detail. Israel had failed to live rightly before God, so God rejected Jerusalem, which was the symbol of his commitment to the nation Israel. However, some within Jerusalem would escape judgement because of their faithfulness to God. God was going to preserve a spiritual 'remnant'.

Chapters 2-5 explained the situation within Israel and the reasons for judgement. Chapter 6 presented God the king. The combination of Israel's sinfulness and God's kingship meant devastating judgement for rebellious Israel. But chapter 6 also held out hope. God promised that in spite of his judgement a stump would remain. The stump probably represents Isaiah and his band of followers—the true Israelites who still wanted to listen to God.

Today's chapter (Isaiah 11) is part of a section of the book (Isaiah 7-12) focusing on the reign of Ahaz, King of Judah. When challenged to trust God, Ahaz failed. Instead of turning to God, he turned to Assyria for help when he was attacked by Syria and Israel (the northern kingdom).

In response to Ahaz, Isaiah prophesied both judgement and salvation. God promised to bring Assyria to destroy the nation but also to prove his trustworthiness by rescuing the righteous and by providing a king who would rule rightly.

Read Isaiah 11.

1. In chapter 11, Isaiah concentrates on one particular figure. Summarize what the passage says about who he is and what he will do.

Where will he come from?	
What will he be like?	
What spirit will rest on him?	
What will he do?	

2. A number of the people or groups mentioned in this passage are important players in Old Testament action. For this reason we have supplied a short glossary below of the more important ones. For each group, describe the prophecies about it in Isaiah 11:12-16.

   - **Ammon and Moab:** Ammon and Moab were the sons of Lot born as a result of the incest between Lot and his daughters. Both nations descended from these men were a constant source of aggravation and temptation to Israel during the journey to the promised land, and its conquest and settlement. Moabites are specifically excluded from Israel (even though Ruth was a Moabitess) and the prophets often single out both nations as people whom God will judge severely.

Prophecies:

- **Assyria:** One of the 'big' nations in Old Testament history (along with Egypt, Babylon and Persia). It was the dominant power as far as Israel was concerned during the time of the kings of Judah and Israel.

  Prophecies:

- **Edom:** Isaac, the son of Abraham, married Rebecca. They had twin sons—Esau (also known as Edom) and Jacob (also known as Israel). There was continual tension between the two brothers and the two nations descended from them.

  Prophecies:

- **Ephraim:** He was the second son of Joseph, the son of Jacob. His descendants became one of the most prestigious of the twelve tribes of Israel. It was the Ephraimite, Jeroboam, who was responsible for splitting the ten northern tribes, including Ephraim, from the southern tribes during the reign of Rehoboam. The prophets often use 'Ephraim' as an alternative expression for 'Israel'.

  Prophecies:

- **Judah:** One of the sons of Jacob and therefore one of the tribes of Israel. Judah is the tribe from which King David and all the kings of the southern kingdom come and, for this reason, 'Judah' is often used to describe the whole southern kingdom.

  Prophecies:

- **Philistia:** The Philistines are descended from Ham, the son of Noah. Abraham and Isaac had reasonably good relationships with the Philistines. During the period of the judges and monarchy in Israel, the Philistines were very aggressive.

  Prophecies:

3. How is 11:1-9 different from 11:10-16? What does the second half of the chapter add to our understanding of what the 'shoot of Jesse' will accomplish?

4. (Optional) It is often easier to remember passages such as Isaiah 11:10-16 by visualizing them. On the map supplied, draw the action described in these verses. If necessary, consult some of the maps in the back of your Bible or out of a Bible dictionary in order to work out where some of the places are.

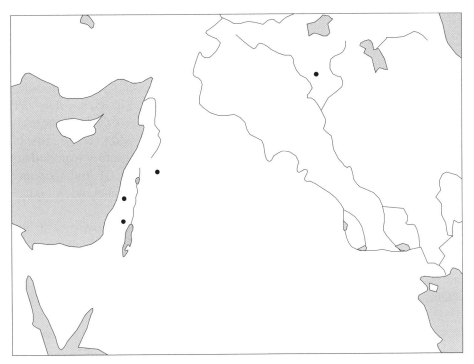

The stump

In our last study on Isaiah 6, we looked at the whole idea of God as king. The Old Testament often talks about the *manner* in which God rules. It tells us that God's kingship is not harsh or tyrannical but full of justice, mercy, compassion and faithfulness. God's rule is a loving rule—he always has the best interests of his subjects in mind (see Ps 145:8-16).

When God appointed kings over Israel, his intention was always that their rule would be exercised in dependence upon the rule of God and that it should reflect his style of leadership. God's kings were not to be ruthless, dominating tyrants who harshly subjugated their people. Rather, they were to be just, compassionate, merciful, loving and good. The kings of Israel were to be servants of their people, always having their best interests in mind. This was the ideal to which the Old Testament looked (see Deut 17:14-20; Psalm 72; Ezekiel 34). It is paraded before us in 2 Samuel 5-7, in the story of David's coronation. Here we see God's united people in the presence of God (symbolized by the temple), in God's city and under the rule of God's king. This is God's dream for his people.

Isaiah 1-12 (and huge slabs of the Old Testament) tells us about the failure of Israelite kings. Their rule did not measure up to expectations and God's dream was shattered. Isaiah pictures the dream as a stump in Isaiah 6. This stump is a monument to God's ideal for his people and his kings.

In chapter 11, Isaiah takes up this language of a stump. He talks of a new shoot from "the stump of Jesse". Jesse was King David's father and so this shoot from the stump is a way of talking about a new king.

The dream fulfilled

In Mark 10:32-45, we are told of Jesus heading towards his certain death. The disciples seem to screen out the possibility of suffering and instead concentrate on the expected glorification of their leader. James and John, in particular, wish to be there when Jesus is glorified and they wish to have positions of power and authority.

Jesus uses the moment to explain what his rule will be like. He will not be like the Gentile rulers who lord it over people. Rather he will be the one who serves by giving his life as a ransom for many. Jesus does what no human being, not even a king of Israel, had done. He submits to the rule of God, and he exercises the rule of God *under* the rule of God. He fulfils the sort of expectations expressed in Isaiah 11 and therefore makes the results pictured in Isaiah 11:6-9 possible.

Given life as we experience it, the promises of such passages as Isaiah 11 can seem a long way off and almost unimaginable. God calls us, however, to line ourselves up with his purposes and his promises, even when they do seem so distant and unreachable. He calls us to mimic the great ones of faith.

Now faith is the assurance of things hoped for, the conviction of things not seen. For by it the people of old received their commendation …

Therefore, since we are surrounded by so great a cloud of witnesses, let us also lay aside every weight, and sin which clings so closely, and let us run with endurance the race that is set before us, looking to Jesus, the founder and perfecter of our faith, who for the joy that was set before him endured the cross, despising the shame, and is seated at the right hand of the throne of God. (Heb 11:1-2, 12:1-2)

» Implications

• Imagine you were commissioned to write a press release on the arrival of the person in chapter 11. What would you say?

• Can you imagine such a situation as that depicted in verses 6-9 ever existing?

  ◦ If not, why not?

  ◦ If so, when?

• What do you look for in an ideal world?

- From Isaiah 11 and Mark 10:35-45, what is God's ideal world like?

- What changes will you need to make to line yourself up with God's dream? To put it another way, if you long for God's ideal world, how is it going to affect your life here and now?

» Give thanks and pray

- Spend some time giving thanks to God for the kind of world that he will one day create through his great king, Jesus.
- Pray that Jesus will return soon and that we will all be ready to meet him.

HOW TO INSULT GOD

[ISAIAH 36-37]

The situation in Israel

SO FAR IN OUR STUDY OF ISAIAH, we have been doing something that is increasingly rare in our society—reading poetry. Chapters 36-39 are very different. Although there is some poetry in this section, most of it is the dramatic history of a battle between two kings. (Much of the material contained in these chapters is identical to that found in 2 Kings 18-20.)

The king of Judah at the time was Hezekiah. Hezekiah was of a different mind to his predecessor, Ahaz. Although willing to pay tribute to foreigners, he was not willing to sell his soul. He engaged in religious reforms and even tried to reconstruct a true Israel consisting of both northern and southern kingdoms.

However, this was a time when Assyrian domination was at its height. Sennacherib had taken over the Assyrian throne. He found himself faced with signs of rebellion in the West (Merodach-Baladan in Babylon) and in the South (Egypt).

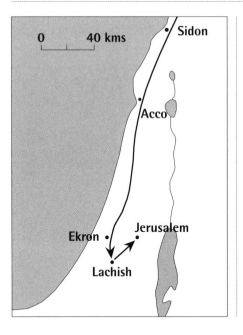

Against the advice of Isaiah, Hezekiah was one of these rebels. He withheld tribute from Sennacherib. Isaiah denounced the rebellion and Sennacherib acted to subdue all resistance.

Sennacherib took 46 of Judah's cities, used Lachish as a base of operations, and laid siege to Jerusalem. According to his own history books, he shut up Hezekiah "like a bird in a cage". This is the period addressed by Isaiah 36-39.

Read Isaiah 36–37.

1. Fill in the following table.

	Main statements and/or events
The Rabshakeh's first speech (36:4-10)	
The Rabshakeh's second speech (36:13-20)	
Hezekiah's reaction (37:1-4)	
Isaiah's reaction (37:5-7)	

The Rabshakeh's third speech (37:8-13)	
Hezekiah's reaction (37:14-20)	
God's response (37:21-38)	

2. Summarize what is said about God in these chapters.

3. What are the possible reasons for Sennacherib's amazing statement in 36:10?

Agreeing with the enemy

THE SPEECHES OF THE RABSHAKEH come across as very powerful and confident. However, much of his first speech actually agrees with what Isaiah himself has been saying! For example:

- It talks about true and false confidence, and questions where Israel puts its confidence.
- It talks about the strategic reasoning that Israel used to justify rebellion against Assyria and questions it.

- It condemns reliance upon Egypt's capacity and desire to support a rebellion against Assyria (Isaiah 30-31).
- It suggests that God himself is ultimately responsible for the Assyrian invasion.

In short, the Rabshakeh's speech echoes God's feelings—Hezekiah is wrong. His trust is falsely placed and he is far too confident of the results of his actions.

Look back over Isaiah 36–37.

4. How did Sennacherib view God and his people? What specific things does he say about God?

5. What is he trying to persuade the people of God to do?

6. As we have seen above, Isaiah had prophesied that Assyria would be God's instrument in judging Israel. Why doesn't this judgement happen here?

7. What specific things does God say about Sennacherib?

8. What does this tell you about the character of God?

Not just another god

IN THIS PASSAGE, A NUMBER OF things are revealed about God and the response that we should make to him.

The God of Israel is not merely the *creator* of all the earth. He is also *sovereign* over it. He directs history and judges the nations and their kings. He is not bullied by human kings.

God is not 'just another god'. The gods of the nations could not stop Assyria—but then they were not gods but only wood and stone, fashioned by human hands. However, the living God fashions humans and directs them by his hands.

God is *jealous* and *holy* and he defends his name, character and reputation. When we say, "hallowed be your name" in the Lord's Prayer, we are actually asking God to do this—to act as a holy God and to defend his name against those who profane it and so insult him.

Propaganda

In these chapters, Sennacherib puts himself in the place of God, insulting God by claiming that he can give Hezekiah and the people of Jerusalem everything that God can give (especially notice the promises given by Sennacherib in 36:16-17 and their similarity to the blessings of the covenant promised by God in Deuteronomy 8:6-9 and 1 Kings 4:25). He is wielding words as weapons of power and using them to present a challenge to both Hezekiah and God.

Hezekiah faces a stark choice: to listen to the words of Sennacherib and trust him to supply all his needs and desires, or to listen to the word of God and trust him. Sennacherib's words are designed to undermine the faith of God's chosen people.

The challenge to God is this: "Whose word is most powerful? Who can give Israel what she really desires—peace and prosperity?"

In the story, God demonstrates whose word is most powerful by actually using his word. It accomplishes what God intends, which is more than Sennacherib's word did.

In our day, there are many who promise the sorts of things God promises. To such people God speaks his alternative word—the word about Christ. He assures us that only in Jesus will God's promises be realized. On the flip side, God's word about Jesus will reveal all human pretensions for what they are—empty propaganda.

» Implications

- How and when do people in our own day insult God in similar ways to Sennacherib?

- As Christians we are urged to put our complete confidence in Christ and his death for us. In your experience what can people do or say to undermine this confidence?

- How will God respond to those who challenge him and his word, and undermine our confidence in his Son?

- How should we react to God's promised response?

» Give thanks and pray

- Pray for those that you can think of who insult God in our world. Ask God to help them see the truth and to repent and turn to Jesus.
- Pray for your church that people will be able to see through untruth and cling to their confidence in Jesus.

THE GOD OF ALL COMFORT

[ISAIAH 40]

A different world

ISAIAH 40 IS LIKE A COOL BREEZE at the end of a scorching day. The mood of its opening verses contrasts so starkly with the judgement and hardship of the preceding section that we feel like we have entered a different world.

We have. Chapters 40-55 are addressed to the nation living in exile in a foreign land. The exile left very deep scars on the Israelite national spirit. Some of these scars are captured in Isaiah 40:27 where the call of the Israelites is recorded. As far as they are concerned, God is defeated or has at least forgotten them. They are suffering alone and God has disregarded their cause.

Read Psalm 137 and Isaiah 40.

1. Psalm 137 is a psalm written about the exile. Describe the experience of the Israelites in exile. What would they have been feeling?

2. Read the verses listed below from Isaiah 40. (If you are meeting in a group, have one person read them out in a loud, proclaiming voice.) What response (emotional and intellectual) would the Israelites in exile have had to each of these proclamations?

- 40:1-2

- 40:6-8

- 40:9-11

- 40:12-14

- 40:15-17

- 40:18-26

- 40:27-31

3. What does each of these verses tell us about God and humanity?

4. What appears to be God's purpose in telling his people these things?

5. What is God promising to do?

Can God be trusted?

IN ISAIAH 40, THE PROPHET IS TOLD to proclaim that God is about to prepare a way out of exile. God himself will dramatically and publicly intervene in history and lead his people through the desert to Palestine.

On being commanded to cry out (v. 6) the prophet sums up the depression of his people and yells back at God:

> A voice says, "Cry!"
> And I said, "What shall I cry?"
> All flesh is grass,
> and all its beauty is like the
> flower of the field.

> The grass withers, the flower fades
> when the breath of the LORD
> blows on it;
> surely the people are grass.
> (Isa 40:6-7)

In other words, Isaiah is asking God: "What on earth can I say to a people who are so desperate and depressed and who feel that their situation is hopeless?"

God's response is recorded in verse 8 —yes, the people are in a desperate situation, but God's word of promise still stands. Unlike grass and flowers, it doesn't wither or fade. Therefore, Isaiah is commanded to comfort God's people, speaking words of comfort and deliverance to them.

The second half of the chapter (40:12-31) is based around the cry of 40:27. The people of God feel deserted by him. They are tempted to abandon God or, at least, charge him with unfaithfulness. God's response is to say that Israel is wrong. Israel should stop grumbling and complaining and instead should turn to trust in him. If they do then God gives them his word that he will not let them down but will rescue them, and the possibilities that will open up for them will outstrip their wildest dreams. The future will be theirs.

Read Isaiah 40:12–31.

6. Find three reasons why Israel is wrong to doubt God's faithfulness.

-

-

-

THE PRINCIPLE OF THE CHAPTER IS clear. God keeps his word. His reputation as God depends on his faithfulness to his word. At times his people will not understand his workings in history and will be tempted to charge him with unfaithfulness, but an examination of his ways and a trust in his word will find him to be trustworthy. God's ways may not always be understood but he can be trusted. He doesn't get tired, take holidays or drop his commitments.

Jesus and Isaiah 40

Read Isaiah 40:3–5 and Luke 3:1–6.

7. What is the difference between the two prophecies?

8. How does John the Baptist see Isaiah 40 being fulfilled?

THE LANGUAGE OF ISAIAH 40 IS BOLD and striking. Given the desperate situation they were in, the Israelites understood it to refer to a literal exodus of the nation from Babylon. History, however, never matched the grandeur of passages such as Isaiah 40-55 and other exilic prophecies which describe this new exodus. Perhaps this is because what was spoken about in Isaiah 40, while firstly directed to a *physical* exile, primarily spoke about a *spiritual* reality, a redemption that God would accomplish.

2 Corinthians 1:20 tells us that Jesus is the 'Yes' to all the promises of God. He is the guarantee that God will live up to his word. We can understand this from Isaiah 40 in a number of ways. In the first place, in Jesus, God does indeed come and accomplish redemption for his people and for the whole world through Jesus' death for sin.

In the second place, God understands our sense of abandonment. On the cross, Jesus experienced abandonment by God. Yet in the agony of that moment he trusted God, committing his future into God's hands. Three days later he was raised by God. His trust in God was vindicated, but perhaps just as importantly, God's faithfulness to his word and promise was proved true.

He gives power to the faint,
and to him who has no might
he increases strength.
Even youths shall faint and be
weary,
and young men shall fall
exhausted;

but they who wait for the Lord
shall renew their strength;
they shall mount up with
wings like eagles;
they shall run and not be weary;
they shall walk and not faint.
(Isa 40:29-31)

» Implications

- In what situations have you felt deserted by God?

- Basing your answers on Isaiah 40 and its fulfilment in Jesus, in these situations what does God:

  - tell us about himself?

  - tell us he will do?

  - tell us to do?

- What actions can you take to respond to what God tells us to do?

» Give thanks and pray

- Give thanks to God for his displays of faithfulness. Thank him for keeping his word and sending Jesus and fulfilling his promises.
- Pray for those you know and, more generally, for those in your church who are feeling deserted or abandoned by God. Pray that they will hear God speaking clearly of his love and care in the death and resurrection of Jesus.

THE SERVANT OF GOD

[ISAIAH 40-55]

FOR MANY CHRISTIANS, THESE chapters contain their favourite Bible prophecies. They reveal themes and characters easily recognizable in the New Testament. It has long been acknowledged that there are a number of passages in Isaiah 40-55 that have a common theme and focus—a person called 'the servant of the LORD'. Each of the passages says different things about the servant.

Read Isaiah 42:1-4, 49:1-6, 50:4-9, 52:13-53:12.

1. Read each of the songs and fill in the diamonds. Highlight the major emphasis in each song by shading in that diamond.

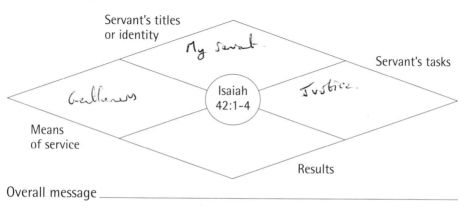

Servant's titles or identity — *My servant.*

Servant's tasks — *Justice.*

Means of service — *Gentleness*

Isaiah 42:1-4

Results

Overall message _____

_____

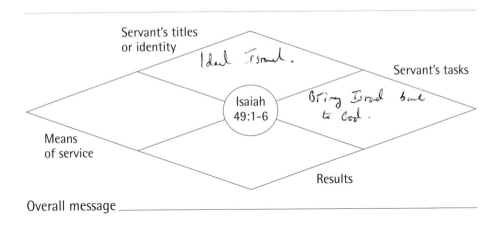

Servant's titles or identity: Ideal Israel.

Servant's tasks: Bring Israel back to God.

Means of service

Isaiah 49:1-6

Results

Overall message _____

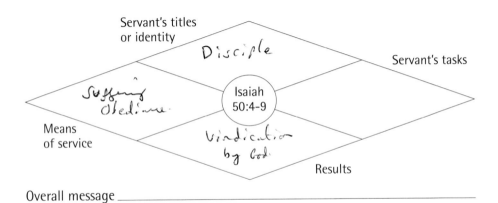

Servant's titles or identity: Disciple

Servant's tasks

Means of service: Suffering Obedience.

Isaiah 50:4-9

Vindication by God.

Results

Overall message _____

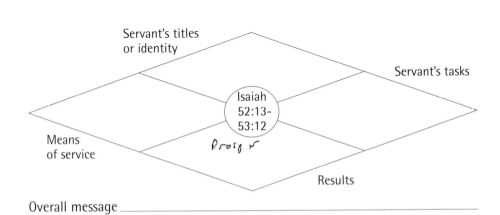

Servant's titles or identity

Servant's tasks

Means of service: Prosper

Isaiah 52:13-53:12

Results

Overall message _____

Since these passages are so important we have supplied a full analysis of them in an appendix at the back of the book. Don't automatically assume we are right and you are wrong if you find some differences with our analysis.

Corporate personality

'CORPORATE PERSONALITY' IS A phrase used by theologians to talk about the way the Bible speaks about one person representing many people. Probably the most famous example in the Bible is in Romans 5, where Paul seems to argue that all humanity existed in Adam and sinned in Adam. In these servant passages in Isaiah, the servant sometimes seems to be a particular individual but in other places seems to be the nation of Israel.

2. Find some examples from these passages of the servant being a particular person and of the servant being the nation of Israel. Why do you think the writer identifies the servant as both?

Read Isaiah 53:4–12.
3. Note down key ideas that are repeated throughout the passage, grouping them together under appropriate headings e.g. 'Suffering', 'Righteousness'.

4. Try to summarize the passage in a single sentence.

The history of the world: Part 1

THE BOOK OF ISAIAH REVEALS TO US a crucial stage in God's purposes for his world. Up to this point, the Bible could be summarized in the manner outlined below.

1. God created the world for his glory and purposes. Within this world, he created men and women to carry out his purposes, to rule the earth under his rule (Genesis 1-2). As we know, we humans failed to live up to the purpose God has for us (Genesis 3).

2. The book of Genesis shows how God called out one nation from all humanity—Abraham and his descendants, Israel (Gen 12:1-3). Though the whole earth was his, this nation was especially selected to be God's people and it was God's intention that through them the whole earth would be blessed.

3. This nation also failed to live up to expectations. By the Spirit of God, the prophets began to understand that Israel's task would not be fulfilled by the nation as a whole but by a godly remnant within the nation.

4. In Isaiah 40-55, this remnant is further reduced to one godly individual. One individual will do what all the others had failed to do. In so doing, he will atone for all the sin of those who should have fulfilled God's mandate, but didn't.

5. The fulfilment of God's mandate by one ideal Israelite will, in turn, enable all Israel to fulfil its mandate to the whole world and indeed, to all creation. Subsequent chapters of Isaiah therefore go on to speak of 'servants', rather than one servant (Isa 65:13-16), and of God restoring his creation (Isa 65:17ff).

People have suggested a number of historical figures that the servant might be (e.g. Isaiah the prophet himself, Zerubbabel, etc.), but none is without problems. The New Testament writers had no doubt about the One in whom the servant passages were fulfilled—it was Jesus. We can see this in passages such as Acts 8:26-35 and Philippians 2:5-11. Jesus is the servant who is obedient to the point of death and who thereby atones for the sins of the world, the One with whom God is pleased and whom God exalts to the highest place of honour.

The gospel in full

The servant passages can, therefore, be seen as an Old Testament summary of the gospel. The complete diagram, taking into account the fulfilment of these passages in Jesus (and in the rest of the New Testament) can be seen below.

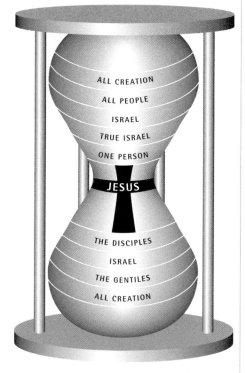

The New Testament records the second half of the story for us. In Jesus, what Israel had failed to do is accomplished. Twelve Jewish disciples are gathered around him, representing true Israel. Within the Gospels we see these twelve on a mission to the rest of Israel, calling the nation to return to God and return to his purpose for them—that they might be the source of blessing to all the nations.

Acts tells us how the Gentiles respond to the gospel—many receive God's purposes gladly and seek to present the gospel to all the known world. Romans 8 pictures a time when, as a result of the gospel, creation itself will be set free from its bondage to slavery. Revelation pictures a new heavens and a new earth where righteousness finally dwells (cf. 2 Pet 3:13) and where God's ideal is finally met. All this flows from Jesus, the one man who did what all human beings did not do and who enabled all mankind to be forgiven for their failure.

We are now part of God's purposes for his world. It is through us and our sharing of the gospel with others that the work of Christ is made known to the world—people are brought back into the relationship with God that he intended us to enjoy. Eventually, the creation itself will be set free from its bondage to decay and brought into the "freedom of the glory of the children of God" (Rom 8:21).

» Implications

Read Acts 8:26–35.

- Pretend you are Philip. What would you have told the eunuch after explaining that the passage was about Jesus?

- While you may or may not have the same evangelistic opportunities as Philip in Acts 8, when do you have opportunities to naturally introduce Jesus into the conversation?

- Who are the people you would like to have opportunities to talk to about Jesus?

- What would you like to tell them?

» Give thanks and pray

- Give thanks to God that Jesus became a servant. Praise God for his forgiveness of our sins.
- Spend time praying for the people that you have listed in the questions above. Ask God to provide you with opportunities to speak with them about Jesus and the right words to say. It would be a great idea to spend some time each week praying for this group of people.

GOD'S RICHEST BANQUET

[ISAIAH 55]

Banquets and salvation

IF WE ARE PRESENTED WITH TWO menus, one a basic survival diet and the other a banquet, unless we have an eating disorder there is no doubt which one we will choose. We only need the basics, but we all long for richness and fullness.

The image of the banquet is a good picture of the human situation. Most of you who read these studies have the basics of life—you have enough (usually, more than enough) to survive. But, paradoxically, for all of us this isn't enough. We long for more, and spend our life searching for fulfilment in a variety of ways: in relationships, pleasure, sex, money, sport, prestige, knowledge, recognition, success and the like.

However, our bitter experience is that these things constantly let us down. Relationships are terminated by death, friends let us down or move on, pleasure doesn't last, money runs out, knowledge is never-ending, prestige and recognition are transitory. The outcome is that we humans will always long for something more. And we do so for good reason, because God has made us for more. He has made us for fullness; for life in abundance.

Read Isaiah 55:1–13.

1. What is God offering?

2. Who is he offering it to? (List their characteristics.)

3. How is it received?

4. Why does he offer it?

5. What guarantees are there that he will actually do as he says?

Read Romans 3:21–26.

6. Which of the principles of salvation seen in Isaiah 55 are also seen in Paul's explanation of the gospel given here?

The Bible and salvation

IN OUR LAST STUDY WE LOOKED AT the 'servant songs' in Isaiah, noting that they reached their climax in the final song in chapter 53. A strong argument can be put forward that chapters 54 and 55 are not separate passages but a continuation of the song.

We were told in Isaiah 53 that the servant's suffering brings wholeness and healing to Israel. She becomes again what she should be—"a light to the nations". In chapter 54, the writer tells us, using a variety of terms and allusions to biblical covenants, that all God's promises will climax in the work of the servant. He will bring a new covenant, which will be centred on a restored and exalted Zion. This language continues on into chapter 55 where, in particular, language from the covenant with David is picked up.

We could summarize the message of salvation given in Isaiah 55 in point form:

- People in the world are in rebellion against God.
- What God offers is only for those who see their need.
- What God offers is fullness of life.
- The offer being made is a free offer.
- Any person can receive this offer by (1) listening to the word God speaks, and (2) responding to it by turning away from an independent attitude and lifestyle.
- God says that his word about salvation is dependable and effective.

Salvation is described in similar ways throughout the Old and New Testaments. Salvation is initiated by God, carried out in his sovereign freedom, and not forced upon people, but offered. The Bible's picture is that this offer of salvation reaches its peak in the person, ministry and work of Jesus. In Jesus, God speaks a dependable and effective word of salvation to a world set against him.

» Implications

- In what situations have you doubted your salvation?

- Which of the principles mentioned in Isaiah 55 gives most help to us when we find ourselves doubting our salvation?

- What response does God require of us when we doubt?

» Give thanks and pray

- Give thanks to God that the certainty of our salvation lies not in us but in the grace and work of God.
- Pray for yourself and those that you know, that God might keep giving you confidence in your knowledge of him through Jesus.

GOD'S FUTURE WORLD

[ISAIAH 64:8–66:6]

Back to the beginning

DURING THESE STUDIES, WE HAVE continually found ourselves going back to Genesis and the beginning of humanity. This is because the Bible continually views history from this perspective. In the Bible, the future is to be viewed by looking backwards— the past shows us the shape of things to come. It continually hints at the future because it shows us God's plans and character. And since he is God, the future will eventually match his expectations.

The situation presented in Genesis 1-2 shows us humanity as it should be. We could summarize it by saying that God's goal for humanity is that we:

- live in right relationship with him (i.e. dependent upon his loving rule)

- live in right relationship with each other
- live in right relationship with our environment.

Genesis 3 shows us how far short of the ideal humanity falls. At the end of this chapter, the relationship between God and mankind is shattered, as is the relationship between one human being and another (Adam and Eve, soon followed by Cain and Abel in Genesis 4) and the relationship between humans and the environment in which they live (e.g. thorns and thistles, etc.).

From this point on, therefore, God's actions in history are directed towards returning to the ideal situation of humans living dependently upon him, in harmony with each other and in harmony with the environment in which he has placed them.

The whole of the book of Isaiah is about this movement from human failure to God's ideal world. As we have seen, the book opens with condemnation of Judah's rebellion against God (see study 1). Much of what follows is about how God will judge his people (and the surrounding nations) for their pride and arrogance, and their failure to trust in him as the true king of all the world (see study 3). However, Isaiah's proclamation of judgement is constantly intermingled with promises of salvation and comfort (as we saw in studies 4 and 6). God's plan is not only to judge his people for their rejection of him, but to ultimately restore a remnant of them to fellowship with himself, to worship him in truth, to live in harmony with one another and with their world.

Read Isaiah 64:8–66:6.

1. Isaiah 64:8-65:7 concerns a breakdown in relationship. Each party has accusations against the other. What are those accusations:

   - against God?

   - against the nation?

2. There are two different responses to God that are recorded in Isaiah 65. Draw pictures or diagrams that illustrate the two different groups and the consequences of the decisions they make about God.

3. God promises a new world. What are the bad things of the present age that Isaiah says will be fixed up in the new world/age of the future?

4. According to Isaiah 65:1-66:6, on what basis can people be part of a restored future world?

5. In that world, what is God's attitude to his restored people?

The truth about God

MANY OF US CAN REMEMBER A period when our lives were dominated by a particular goal. We lived, slept, and breathed that particular thing until it was reached. Most of us can also remember what we did when (if!) that goal was successfully reached. We punched the air, leapt for joy and celebrated. Setting goals and reaching them is one of the things that gives us great delight.

The God of the Bible also sets goals. As we have seen, he has a particular goal for his creation. Every now and then the Bible also records God's reactions to his goal being successfully reached in his people. In Isaiah 65, we are told that he is glad, that he rejoices, that he takes delight. When the remnant is purified and God restores his people, he is said to burst into song (Zeph 3:17). God takes great pleasure when he finds people who live before him in the way that he always intended them to live.

There is a magnificent picture of this in Luke 15. Here we are told of a father who is abused and mistreated by his son.

The son decides to return to his father's house. His father sees him coming at a distance and does something unheard of for an elderly man of status and reputation—in his great compassion, he forgets all decorum and runs out to meet his son, throwing his arms around him and kissing the one who had disgraced him. This is followed by a great celebration as the father throws a party for his lost son who has returned.

Most of us have a twisted view of God that paints him as an ogre waiting to pounce upon us for the slightest thing. This is not the picture presented in the Bible. God is one who is long-suffering, who risks all to forgive us, who actually sends his son into the world to die for us in order that our relationship with him might be restored. He is a God who loves the world so much that he gives his only Son so that whoever believes in him can have life of an eternal quality and quantity.

Like the father in Luke 15, God will let us go away from him, but only with great sadness. His desire is that we repent.

He wants to rejoice over us with singing.

Isaiah 65 tells us that God's delight in his people has tangible consequences. When people humble themselves, repent and tremble at his word, his generosity overflows and he creates for them a whole new environment characterized by peace, harmony, longevity and safety. In other words, God creates a new heavens and a new earth in which righteousness dwells (cf. 2 Pet 3:13).

This whole image of God's delight in his people is captured in the closing chapters of the book of Revelation where God is said to throw a huge wedding feast for his Son. The participants in this feast—those who have received the benefits of Christ's death—will be the inhabitants of God's restored Eden. Here there will be people who:

- live in right relationship with him (i.e. are dependent upon his loving rule)
- live in right relationship with each other
- live in right relationship with the environment in which he has placed them.

» Implications

- On what basis can you be part of a restored future world?

- What is God's attitude to you as a member of that restored world?

- What implications does this have for you in terms of your attitudes and actions?

- From this study, what is the basis for our joy in being Christian? What does a lack of joy suggest?

» Give thanks and pray

- Give thanks to God for all the richness and joy that he promises us in heaven.
- Ask God to help you to live now in light of that future. Pray in particular for him to change your attitudes and actions where they need to change.

» THE HISTORICAL CONTEXT OF ISAIAH 1-39

ISAIAH PREACHED DURING A crucial time in Israel's history. He ministered during the reigns of the Judean kings Uzziah, Jotham, Ahaz and Hezekiah (Isa 1:1).

At the time of Uzziah, the dominant power in the world of the Ancient Near East was Assyria. It was a time of relative peace and prosperity because the King of Assyria was busy with unrest at home, and the other nearby power-broker Syria (sometimes designated by Damascus, its capital) was seriously weakened.

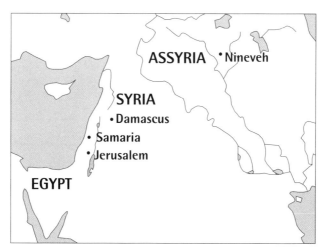

The death of Uzziah marked the end of this era. His son Jotham's reign coincided with fresh Assyrian campaigns under the leadership of Tiglath-pileser III. The maps on the next page outline the series of events as they affected the southern kingdom of Judah, where Isaiah was prophesying. By this time in Israel's history, the nation had been divided into two kingdoms. 'Israel' is generally (but not always) used to refer to the northern kingdom while 'Judah' is used to refer to the southern kingdom.

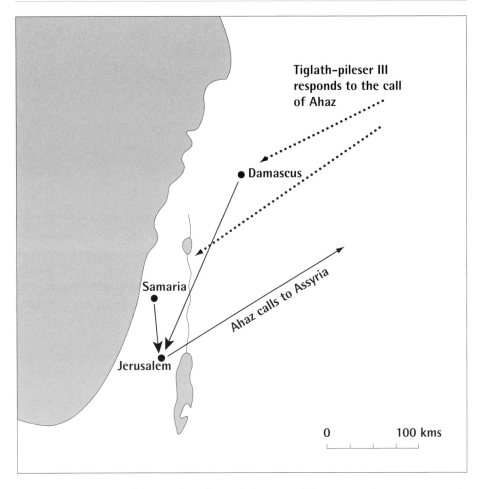

Stage 1: Damascus and the northern kingdom of Israel put pressure on Jotham and his young successor, Ahaz, to join them in rebellion against Assyria.

Stage 2: Isaiah advised Judah to remain neutral. In response, the kings of Israel and Syria marched up to Jerusalem in order to depose Ahaz and replace him with a puppet king, the son of Tabeel (2 Kgs 16:5-6; cf. Isa 7:6). Judah incurred heavy losses (2 Chr 28:5-8), but Ahaz managed to avoid being deposed (2 Kgs 16:5).

Stage 3: The pressure became too much for Ahaz. He sought to preserve his throne by submitting himself as a vassal to Assyria and by offering a huge sum of money (2 Kgs 16:7-9; 2 Chr 28:16; Isa 7:1-8:18). In response, Tiglath-pileser devastated Damascus in 732 and invaded Israel as far south as Galilee (2 Kgs 15:29).

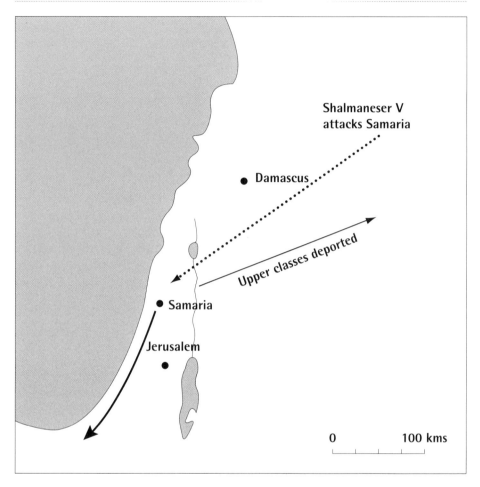

Stage 4: Tiglath-pileser was succeeded by his son, Shalmaneser V. Israel took this as an opportunity to transfer allegiances to Egypt. In response, Shalmaneser laid siege to Samaria (capital of Israel), defeated it, and deported the upper classes (2 Kings 17).

The reign of Ahaz comes in for sharp criticism from the prophets. He sacrifices his child to the god Molech (2 Kgs 16:3), reacts cynically to Isaiah (Isa 7:12), subjects the nation to Assyria and therefore adopts an Assyrian-style altar for the Jerusalem temple (2 Kgs 16:10-16) and allows the practice of much social injustice (Isa 3:13-15, 5:8-13; Mic 2:1-10). It is the reign of Ahaz that appears to be the focus of the early chapters of Isaiah.

As can be seen in the later studies, Hezekiah was of a different mind from Ahaz. Although he was willing to pay tribute, he was not willing to sell out to pagan nations.

»THE SERVANT SONGS

THESE DETAILED ANALYSES OF Isaiah 40-55 are included to supplement your own study of the passages. If there are differences between your conclusions and ours, don't automatically assume that we are right and you are wrong—or vice versa! Instead, return to the passages and read them again.

Isaiah 42:1-4

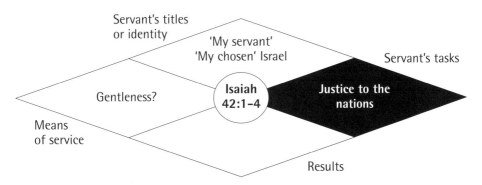

Servant's titles or identity

"My servant" and "my chosen" seem to most naturally refer to the nation of Israel (cf. 41:8-10).

Servant's task

The task is the focus of the first servant song. The servant is to bring forth justice to the nations and establish it in all the earth, and do so in truth. The servant's task, therefore, is to bring about the judgement and salvation of the nations and their willing submission to God (42:6).

Means of service

It is not made clear, but the servant seems to be distinguished by his gentleness (42:2).

Overall message

There is, at the present time, a seemingly unbridgeable gap between Israel's present state—captive in Babylon—and her ultimate destiny—a light to the nations. This is bridged through the figure and mission of the servant.

Isaiah 49:1–6

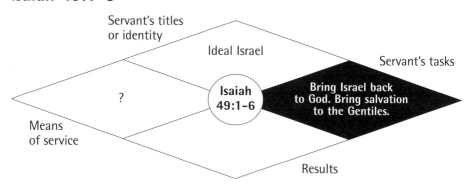

Servant's titles or identity

The servant's identity is revealed in 49:3—Israel. But later verses say the servant has a mission to Israel. The best way to solve this apparent conflict is to recognize that this passage refers to a perfect or ideal Israel within the larger, corrupt nation.

Servant's task

The servant's task is again the focus of the song. His task is both to bring Jacob back to God and to bring salvation to the Gentiles.

Means of service

How this task will be achieved is not made clear in the passage.

Overall message

Here we see 'ideal Israel' at work to turn Israel into whom she should be. The passage ends with the servant's ministry beyond the borders of Israel. He is becoming a 'light to the nations' to the ends of the earth.

Isaiah 50:4–9

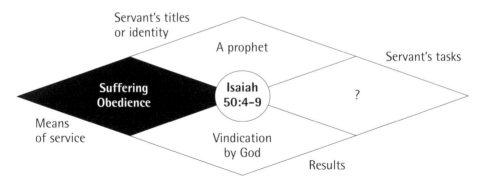

Servant's titles or identity

In this passage, the servant is speaking, which makes it difficult to establish his identity. Prophecy seems to be involved, so it could even be Isaiah speaking. It is safest to say simply that he is a prophet. Notice the contrast between this servant and Israel. Where Israel is rebellious, the servant is obedient. He is therefore a model for those who would fear God (50:10).

Servant's task

The servant accepts his suffering and hopes for vindication—he is unswervingly obedient. Suffering is clearly necessary for the servant's task, but the link between suffering and the task is not explained.

Means of service

The way the servant goes about fulfilling the task is the focus of this song. The servant accepts suffering with unflinching obedience, and he speaks forth God's word.

Results

The servant will be vindicated by God.

Isaiah 52:13–53:12

Servant's titles or identity

The servant is strikingly personal in this passage. His true identity is almost universally unrecognized by those around him.

Servant's task

The link between the servant's task and his suffering is explained—he is to bring the salvation of Israel through his suffering. Two features of this suffering are important: he is smitten by God (53:4) and he suffers on behalf of others (53:9, 12 and elsewhere).

Means of service

Suffering is again the means of justice and salvation. The servant is smitten by God (53:4) and suffers on behalf of others (53:9, 12, etc.).

Results

The results of the servant's suffering are twofold. Firstly, his suffering affects the whole of Israel, bringing healing, restoration and declarations of righteousness. Israel becomes a 'light to the nations'. Secondly, the servant is vindicated by God.

Overall message

This servant song deals with the spiritual need of Israel. It becomes clear that the servant's suffering fulfils his task.

Summary

If we consider the servant songs together, we can construct a multi-layered, composite model of the servant. Isaiah prophesies that the servant will do what Israel was supposed to do. He will listen to God's word, speak God's word and obey God's word. He will suffer on behalf of people who have failed to live rightly before God. Through this suffering, the servant will restore the people to God, bringing wholeness and making the people of God a light to the nations. Finally, the servant will himself be vindicated before God because of his humility, obedience and suffering.

As to the servant's identity, we have three options:

- Was it a figure from Isaiah's time? No one individual seems to fit the full picture.
- Was it a later figure, such as Zerubbabel? It is possible, but we are not given enough information to make it a good guess.
- Was it a much later figure, such as Jesus? The New Testament confirms that this is the case, in passages such as Acts 8:26-40 and Philippians 2:5-11. As Philip told the Ethiopian eunuch, Isaiah was prophesying the good news about Jesus the Suffering Servant.

matthiasmedia

Matthias Media is an evangelical publishing ministry that seeks to persuade all Christians of the Bible-shaped, theological truth of God's purposes in Jesus Christ, and equip them with high-quality resources, so that they will:

- abandon their lives to the honour and service of Christ in daily holiness and decision-making
- pray constantly in Christ's name for the growth of his gospel
- speak the Bible's life-changing word whenever and however they can— in the home, in the world and in the fellowship of his people.

It was in 1988 that we first started pursuing this mission, and in God's kindness we now have more than 300 different ministry resources being used all over the world. These resources range from Bible studies and books through to training courses and audio sermons.

To find out more about our large range of very useful resources, and to access samples and free downloads, visit our website:

www.matthiasmedia.com.au

How to buy our resources

1. Direct from us over the internet:
   – in the US: www.matthiasmedia.com
   – in Australia and the rest of the world: www.matthiasmedia.com.au

2. Direct from us by phone:
   – in the US: 1 866 407 4530
   – in Australia: 1800 814 360
     (Sydney: 9663 1478)
   – international: +61-2-9663-1478

> Register at our website for our **free** regular email update to receive information about the latest new resources, **exclusive special offers**, and free articles to help you grow in your Christian life and ministry.

3. Through a range of outlets in various parts of the world.
   Visit **www.matthiasmedia.com.au/international.php** for details about recommended retailers in your part of the world, including www.thegoodbook.co.uk in the United Kingdom.

4. Trade enquiries can be addressed to:
   – in the US and Canada: sales@matthiasmedia.com
   – in Australia and the rest of the world: sales@matthiasmedia.com.au

Other Interactive and Topical Bible Studies from Matthias Media

Our Interactive Bible Studies (IBS) and Topical Bible Studies (TBS) are a valuable resource to help you keep feeding from God's word. The IBS series works through passages and books of the Bible; the TBS series pulls together the Bible's teaching on topics such as money or prayer. As at February 2009, the series contains the following titles:

Beyond Eden
GENESIS 1-11
Authors: Phillip Jensen and Tony Payne, 9 studies

Out of Darkness
EXODUS 1-18
Author: Andrew Reid, 8 studies

The Shadow of Glory
EXODUS 19-40
Author: Andrew Reid, 7 studies

The One and Only
DEUTERONOMY
Author: Bryson Smith, 8 studies

The Good, the Bad and the Ugly
JUDGES
Author: Mark Baddeley, 10 studies

Famine and Fortune
RUTH
Authors: Barry Webb and David Höhne, 4 studies

Renovator's Dream
NEHEMIAH
Authors: Phil Campbell and Greg Clarke, 7 studies

The Eye of the Storm
JOB
Author: Bryson Smith, 6 studies

The Search for Meaning
ECCLESIASTES
Author: Tim McMahon, 9 studies

Two Cities
ISAIAH
Authors: Andrew Reid and Karen Morris, 9 studies

Kingdom of Dreams
DANIEL
Authors: Andrew Reid and Karen Morris, 9 studies

Burning Desire
OBADIAH AND MALACHI
Authors: Phillip Jensen and Richard Pulley, 6 studies

Warning Signs
JONAH
Author: Andrew Reid, 6 studies

On That Day
ZECHARIAH
Author: Tim McMahon, 8 studies

Full of Promise
THE BIG PICTURE OF THE O.T.
Authors: Phil Campbell and Bryson Smith, 8 studies

The Good Living Guide
MATTHEW 5:1-12
Authors: Phillip Jensen and Tony Payne, 9 studies

News of the Hour
MARK
Authors: Peter Bolt and Tony Payne, 10 studies

Proclaiming the Risen Lord
LUKE 24-ACTS 2
Author: Peter Bolt, 6 studies

Mission Unstoppable
ACTS
Author: Bryson Smith, 10 studies

The Free Gift of Life
ROMANS 1-5
Author: Gordon Cheng, 8 studies

The Free Gift of Sonship
ROMANS 6-11
Author: Gordon Cheng, 8 studies

The Freedom of Christian Living
ROMANS 12-16
Author: Gordon Cheng, 7 studies

Free for All
GALATIANS
Authors: Phillip Jensen and Kel Richards, 8 studies

Walk this Way
EPHESIANS
Author: Bryson Smith, 8 studies

Partners for Life
PHILIPPIANS
Author: Tim Thorburn, 8 studies

The Complete Christian
COLOSSIANS
Authors: Phillip Jensen and Tony Payne, 8 studies

To the Householder
1 TIMOTHY
Authors: Phillip Jensen and Greg Clarke, 9 studies

Run the Race
2 TIMOTHY
Author: Bryson Smith, 6 studies

The Path to Godliness
TITUS
Authors: Phillip Jensen and Tony Payne, 7 studies

From Shadow to Reality
HEBREWS
Author: Joshua Ng, 10 studies

The Implanted Word
JAMES
Authors: Phillip Jensen and Kirsten Birkett, 8 studies

Homeward Bound
1 PETER
Authors: Phillip Jensen and Tony Payne, 10 studies

All You Need to Know
2 PETER
Author: Bryson Smith, 6 studies

The Vision Statement
REVELATION
Author: Greg Clarke, 9 studies

Bold I Approach
PRAYER
Author: Tony Payne, 6 studies

Cash Values
MONEY
Author: Tony Payne, 5 studies

The Blueprint
DOCTRINE
Authors: Phillip Jensen and Tony Payne, 9 studies

Woman of God
THE BIBLE ON WOMEN
Author: Terry Blowes, 8 studies

Kingdom of Dreams
9 studies on Daniel

The lion's den … the fiery furnace … the writing on the wall … the four-headed beast.

The book of Daniel contains some of the Bible's most vivid and unusual stories. It's an exciting read, but a disturbing one too. What are we to make of Daniel's dreams and visions? And what does Daniel have to say to us in our age?

Set during the exile of God's people in Babylon, the book of Daniel gives us a dramatic account of how God provides his people with hope amidst adversity. It's the story of God's faithfulness to those he loves.

Kingdom of Dreams captures the wonders of this part of the Bible, steers a path through the difficult passages, and leaves us in awe of the King of kings.

Warning Signs
6 studies on Jonah

A prophet refuses God's commands, flees across the waters, is thrown overboard by zealous pagan sailors, saved by a giant fish and cast up on a beach.

So begins one of the Bible's most famous stories, one which has intrigued Christian readers for centuries. Is Jonah a Christlike figure, spending three days in the belly of the whale before being sent to save a lost city? Or is he a disobedient sulker whom God teaches a lesson about love and mercy?

Warning Signs unravels the meaning of this short Old Testament book. Andrew Reid follows Jonah's journey to the city of Nineveh. He considers what God might be teaching Jonah through the voyage, and what lessons we ourselves can learn about God's compassion, his power and his patience.

FOR MORE INFORMATION OR TO ORDER CONTACT:

Matthias Media
Telephone: +61-2-9663-1478
Facsimile: +61-2-9663-3265
Email: info@matthiasmedia.com.au
Internet: www.matthiasmedia.com.au

Matthias Media (USA)
Telephone: 1-866-407-4530
Facsimile: 724-964-8166
Email: sales@matthiasmedia.com
Internet: www.matthiasmedia.com

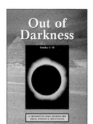

Out of Darkness
8 studies on Exodus 1-18

An oppressed people, a reluctant hero, a cruel and all-powerful dictator.

As the book of Exodus opens, we wonder how God is going to keep his ancient promises to his chosen people. But in his majestic power, God proves himself to be more than a match for Egypt's arrogant king. As God rescues his wayward people, and gathers them to himself at Mt Sinai, we see a stunning picture of God's grace and faithfulness and power and truth. Despite the obstacles, despite the seeming hopelessness of the situation, despite even the sinfulness of those needing rescue, God brings his people out of darkness and into his wonderful light.

Andrew Reid guides us through the extraordinary story of God's rescue of Israel, and shows us how this drama points to the work of Christ.

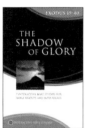

The Shadow of Glory
7 studies on Exodus 19-40

Following on from *Out of Darkness* (Exodus 1-18) comes this next instalment in Andrew Reid's insightful studies on the book of Exodus.

The storyline is simple yet tragic. A gracious God has rescued his people, chosen them to live as his precious nation and graciously given them his law. But an ungracious people has immediately let him down. How can God continue to be gracious, yet be true to his just standard?

Exodus 19-40 is one of the most significant sections of the entire Bible. It not only lays the foundation of God's relationship with his chosen people Israel, but also foreshadows the glorious relationship of God with all humanity through Jesus Christ.

Pathway Bible Guides

Pathway Bible Guides are simple, straightforward, easy-to-read Bible studies, ideal for groups who are new to studying the Bible, or groups with limited time.

We've designed the studies to be short and easy to use, with an uncomplicated vocabulary. At the same time, we've tried to do justice to the passages being

studied, and to model good Bible-reading principles. Pathway Bible Guides are simple without being simplistic; no-nonsense without being no-content.

As at February 2009, the series contains the following titles:

- *Beginning with God* (Genesis 1-12)
- *Getting to Know God* (Exodus 1-20)
- *The Art of Living* (Proverbs)
- *Seeing Things God's Way* (Daniel)
- *Fear and Freedom* (Matthew 8-12)
- *Following Jesus* (Luke 9-12)
- *Peace with God* (Romans)
- *Church Matters* (1 Corinthians 1-7)
- *Standing Firm* (1 Thessalonians)

Getting to Know God
8 simple studies on Exodus 1-20

How can we learn about God and his ways?

In Exodus 1-20 we meet the true and living God who makes and keeps promises, who judges, saves and triumphs, who provides for his people and teaches them his holy ways.

In *Getting to Know God*, Andrew Reid covers the early and momentous chapters of Exodus. He gives us a clear picture of God's character and how we should respond. Leader's notes are included in the booklet.

FOR MORE INFORMATION OR TO ORDER CONTACT:

Matthias Media
Telephone: +61-2-9663-1478
Facsimile: +61-2-9663-3265
Email: info@matthiasmedia.com.au
Internet: www.matthiasmedia.com.au

Matthias Media (USA)
Telephone: 1-866-407-4530
Facsimile: 724-964-8166
Email: sales@matthiasmedia.com
Internet: www.matthiasmedia.com

The Daily Reading Bible

The all-in-one, take-anywhere package to help you feed regularly from God's word.

This popular devotional series is becoming the staple diet for many Christians as they spend time with God. *The Daily Reading Bible* is an all-in-one resource and a good way to get started or keep going in your daily reading of the Bible.

Each volume contains around 60 undated readings. Each reading is designed to take around 15-20 minutes, and contains:

- the full text of the Bible passage
- questions to get you thinking
- 'points to ponder'
- ideas to get you started in prayer.

It's all together in one booklet that you can take with you anywhere—on the train, on the bus, to the park at lunchtime, or to your favourite armchair.

Vol	Contains studies on ...
1	Matthew 5-6, Joshua, 1 Corinthians 1-4
2	1 Corinthians 5-7, Malachi, 'The Trinitarian God'
3	Genesis 1-11, 2 Thessalonians, Hebrews 1-7, 'Jesus, the Coming One'
4	Matthew 8-16, Nehemiah, Hebrews 8-13
5	James, 'The Atonement', Genesis 12-35
6	Ephesians, Lamentations, Proverbs
7	1 Peter, Zechariah, Revelation 1-3, 'Present Suffering'
8	John 1-12, Hosea, 'Words and the power of what, how and why we speak'
9	John 13-21, Isaiah 1-12, Philippians
10	1 Timothy, Exodus 1-18, 'The Christian calling'
11	2 Peter, Genesis 36-50, Ecclesiastes
12	'Elijah', Matthew 1-4, 1 Thessalonians
13	Luke 1-6, Amos, 2 Corinthians
14	Luke 7-9, Micah, Galatians
15	Luke 9-15, Jonah, 2 Timothy
16	Luke 16-19, Job 1-26, 1 Corinthians 8-16
17	Luke 19-24, Job 27-42, 'Church'
18	Acts 1-9, Numbers, Colossians

FOR MORE INFORMATION OR TO ORDER CONTACT:

Matthias Media
Telephone: +61-2-9663-1478
Facsimile: +61-2-9663-3265
Email: info@matthiasmedia.com.au
Internet: www.matthiasmedia.com.au

Matthias Media (USA)
Telephone: 1-866-407-4530
Facsimile: 724-964-8166
Email: sales@matthiasmedia.com
Internet: www.matthiasmedia.com